Preface

Today, we know more about the history of the *Mona Lisa* than ever before. Researchers have an unprecedented grasp of the historical parameters surrounding what is the most famous painting in the Louvre. Engineers, chemists and experts on painting techniques have made great progress in the analysis of the various elements that constitute the renowned painting and the successive phases of their application. The rigorous work of the conservators has given us a precise idea of the condition of the *Mona Lisa* and therefore of its fragility, so that we are more clearly aware of the measures required to ensure its conservation for centuries to come.

Thus, our factual, objective and scientific understanding of the *Mona Lisa* is more comprehensive and more varied than at any time in the past. Curiously enough, however, the fantasies surrounding the painting and its mysteries are also more potent than ever. Even if the painter left plenty of clues to help us understand the *Mona Lisa*, both in his notebooks and in his other works, we still do not know exactly what his deeper motivations were when he composed this painting which is often described as a 'mental self-portrait'. Like all masterpieces, the *Mona Lisa* remains something of a mystery, a universal work freighted with poetry and dreams. As such, it is endlessly open to interpretation.

The job of the Louvre is not to solve the enigma that has surrounded the painting for hundreds of years. Its main duty is to make the work of art available, to ensure that it can be viewed in the best possible conditions. It was with this in mind that we planned the renovation of the Salle des Etats, which now provides the *Mona Lisa* with the most handsome showcase imaginable. Here I would like to pay an admiring homage to Lorenzo Piqueras, the architect who worked on the room. My compliments also go to the oversight body for cultural development at the Louvre for their meticulous work on this project and my special thanks to the keepers in the Department of Paintings - Cécile Scailliérez, Jean Habert and Vincent Pomarède - who monitored the building work and directed the hanging of the Venetian paintings that now surround the *Mona Lisa*. I also wish to express my deepest gratitude to Nippon Television, who financed the successive phases of the renovation of the Salle des Etats.

HENRI LOYRETTE
CHAIRMAN AND DIRECTOR OF THE MUSÉE DU LOUVRE

D1418340

The 'Mona Lisa'

a Model Portrait

Behind the modern-day icon and myth, the 'Mona Lisa' is one of the great masterpieces in the history of art. Leonardo da Vinci's portrait was a model for generations of painters and, in his own oeuvre, represents the culmination of over thirty years of thought and experimentation.

By Fabrice Douar

As a work of art, the *Mona Lisa* has not always had the paragon status we accord it today. And, regarding the latter, could it not be argued that things might have turned out differently if the painting had not been aggressed stolen, satirised and subjected to artistic pastiches throughout the twentieth century, and thus gradually converted into a modern icon? That said, the purpose of this essay is not to understand the mechanics of this process that raised the *Mona Lisa* to the status of supreme masterpiece, but to focus on the qualities that make the painting a landmark in Leonardo da Vinci's oeuvre, and in the history of art in general.

Painted over a period of more than ten years, starting in 1503, the *Mona Lisa* marks a culmination of Renaissance ideas about the rules of representation governing the portrait. Rather than challenge the conventions of the age, it indeed carries forward an ongoing development, which it brings to a high point. The fact that other painters should have been so quick to adopt it as a model tells us that the formal solutions put forward by Leonardo in the *Mona Lisa* represent a kind of consummation, a perfection that everyone was striving for and that he was the first to achieve.

The conditions of the commission

As for the commissioning, making and payment of this painting, there is no information to be found either in Leonardo's prolific writings or in the archives. According to scholars, the most likely hypothesis is that the artist, who was active in Florence from the turn of the sixteenth century, agreed to paint a portrait of the wife of a wealthy Florentine merchant, one Francesco del Giocondo. Some even believe that Giocondo may have commissioned two portraits: one of his young wife, and another – which has disappeared without trace – of himself.

What do we know about the model? Born in 1479, Lisa di Noldo Gherardini married Francesco del Giocondo in 1495 and bore him three children: Piero Francesco, born 23 May, 1496, a daughter about whom we know only that she died on 6 June 1499, and a second son, Andrea, born 1 December 1502. She was of modest

Leonardo da Vinci
Portrait of Lisa Gherardini, or *Mona Lisa* or *La Gioconda*,
1503-1506, oil on wood (poplar), 77 x 53 cm,
Paris, Musée du Louvre.

stock whereas her husband, a wealthy merchant, frequented such important families as the Strozzis and the Donis, and had a family chapel in the prestigious church of the Santissima Annunziata in Florence. In April 1503, a few months after the birth of his second son, Francesco moved the family to a new house. It seems logical that this distinguished figure should have wanted to enlist the services of a famous painter for a portrait of his young wife to adorn his home. Especially when we bear in mind that Leonardo had left the employ of Cesare Borgia and was now relatively free (the commission for *The Battle of Anghiari* was not made until October 1503). Leonardo spent about four years in Florence before leaving for Milan in 1506. In 1513 he was summoned to Rome by Giulio de' Medici. His painting of Mona Lisa was still unfinished and Leonardo certainly had it with him when he travelled to Amboise at the invitation of Francis I in 1516. Francesco del Giocondo would have to wait for his commission.

The composition

But what exactly do we see? A female figure sitting in a loggia with a landscape behind her. Taking up nearly the whole of the painting, the portrait is half-length, in half-profile, the head turned towards the beholder. The woman who looks out at us is calm and collected.

While the representation gives an impression of naturalness and simplicity, its composition is in fact highly complex. To begin with, the painter has placed the figure in a pyramidal structure that stabilises the ensemble by virtue of the wide base on which it rests, but which also sets up an initial upwards movement going from the arms to the head. This movement is echoed by the position of the sitter's body. Above the left arm, placed on the armrest of the chair, and thus indicating that all the lower part of the body is parallel to the picture plane, the bust twists to face the beholder. This movement is continued by the head, which faces us almost frontally, and culminates with the orientation of the gaze, perpendicular to the canvas, engaging the beholder in an intense face-to-face. The counterpart of this spiral movement is the serpentine line that goes from the left arm to the head via the diagonal axis of the shoulders. The loggia where Mona Lisa is sitting plays an important role in setting off the figure and in creating the impression that she is leaning forward. The wall and the two very discreet columns delimit a space within the painting which, by narrowing the frame (like a photographic zoom), compels the beholder to focus on Mona Lisa's face. As a result, this stands out boldly against the landscape in the background. This landscape offers a vista off into the distance, in what is almost an aerial view, and thus offsets the very restricted frontal vision of the foreground, dominated as it is by the seated figure. It presents the beholder with an alternative. Leonardo sets up a constant back-and-forth movement between the fixed, stable foreground and the animation of the landscape. Our

In this painting Leonardo expounds an analogy between nature and the human body in which water is seen as the blood of the earth, with rocks and mountains as its bones, its skeleton. The presence of the bridge in this virgin landscape is a sign of human activity.

'Mona Lisa': a Model Portrait

now captive gaze thus moves endlessly from front to back, destabilised by this network of subtle but effective connections.

There are numerous formal echoes and continuities between the foreground and background, figure and landscape. The hillock on the right thus appears to extend the fabric draped over Lisa's left shoulder. The curls of her hair are echoed in the twists of the path on the left. These interrelations are reinforced by the luminous and chromatic unity of the whole, which, far from distinguishing the figure from the ground, unifies them in the same shady atmosphere. The line of the horizon, deliberately placed high up in the image, heightens the effect of the figure's immersion in its natural surroundings. Further, its height directs our gaze towards Lisa's face, and means that her eyes and forehead stand out strongly against this part of the image occupied only by the 'empty' sky and the peaks of the mountains. Lisa's gaze is underscored by this horizontal and thus stabilises our own gaze at its own level, exerting its captive, penetrating power on us, while keeping us at a 'reasonable' distance.

The position of the hands contributes to this same balance between distance and closeness, to the figure's simultaneous remoteness from and proximity to the spectator. Usually, painters put a parapet in the foreground of their portrait to endow the figure with visual stability while creating a sense of space at the front and thereby instituting a distance, an insuperable barrier between the beholder and the subject of the portrait. Here we have a discreet echo of that parapet in the armrest of the chair on which Mona Lisa is leaning. By getting rid of the parapet, Leonardo invites us to share Lisa's space, to enter the loggia. At the same time, while we may feel physically closer, the position of the hands imposes a 'civil' distance that we cannot move beyond.

Iconography and interpretation

Every work of art is the product of a specific historical context. If certain elements in a painting mystify us, this may well be because we are unaware of the conditions prevailing over its creation, or because we are unfamiliar with the facts needed to understand it. This can sometimes lead to dubious interpretations (think of all the prose – psychoanalytic and otherwise – generated by Mona Lisa's famously 'enigmatic' smile). We need to remember that the Mona Lisa is the product of a dialogue between different worlds, between two different cultural spaces: Leonardo's artistic universe, with his own personal experiments on the one hand and, on the other, the tradition of portraiture, which he took into consideration in making his painting; and the universe of the social group that commissioned the work. The painting had to satisfy the artist's own demands while respecting the firmly established social codes of the Florentine elite at the turn of the sixteenth century, since these to a large extent determined the 'taste' of the patron.

The position of Mona Lisa's hands and her

Mona Lisa's smile and the position of her hands reflect the codes of decorum recommended to young women in Leonardo's day.

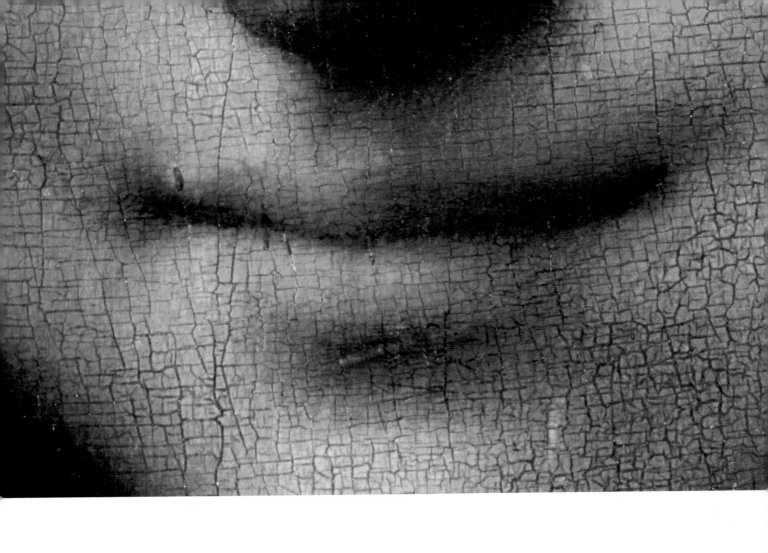

'Mona Lisa': a Model Portrait

smile thus obey the rules of propriety for social conduct recommended to women of that period and laid down in manuals for young girls. The hands here are without the kind of allusive accessory or symbolic attribute usually found in such portraits, and therefore have a moral value in themselves, offering a harmonious combination of sound morals and natural corporeal posture. Similarly, the light black veil over Mona Lisa's hair indicates that she is married and – contrary to the view of those who linked this painting with the death of the Giocondos' daughter – *not* in mourning. In fact, the fine texture of this veil brings to mind the kind of feminine accessory produced by the fashion for dark clothes that is thought to have come from Spain at the beginning of the sixteenth century. All these elements back up the hypothesis that the painting was made to adorn the family home.

Although relatively plain, Mona Lisa's gown also bespeaks her affluence, particularly its low-cut neckline edged with interlacing gold embroidery. Not that the painting is, as one might have expected it to be, an ostentatious portrait of a rich silk merchant's wife. Leonardo has clearly gone beyond this conventional aspect of the genre and developed an analogy between nature and the human being, between macrocosm and microcosm. Water, which, as we know, was one of Leonardo's great scientific interests, is present here in two different ways: moving and alive on the right, where its flow forms a river, and more dormant and calm to the left, where it fills out lakes. Water represents the blood of the earth while, in this scheme of things, rocks and mountains can be likened to its bones, its skeleton. This representation could thus be read as Leonardo's personal allusion to the primitive topography of the Arno which, according to the art historian Daniel Arasse, would then constitute the portrait's imaginary background: '[…] the happy and fertile Lisa del Giocondo, whose youthful, twofold maternity brought joy to the man who commissioned the painting, becomes the incarnation of the earth's vital power.'

Another detail that tells us something about the meaning of this portrait is the bridge on the right, a sign of human activity which might seem surprising in this otherwise virgin landscape. It can be seen to symbolise the passage or transition between two inner states. Related to Mona Lisa, it seems to echo the effect of her smile and signal an inner movement, the life of the soul. The young woman's Italian name, Gioconda, does after all derive from the Latin adjective *jucundus*, meaning serene or pleasant.

Leonardo's other portraits

Modest as its dimensions (77 x 53 cm) may seem by today's standards, Mona Lisa is the biggest of the six surviving portraits painted by Leonardo. In fact, portraits on this scale were a rarity before 1500, the only notable exceptions being the series of *Famous Figures* by Joos van Gent and Pedro Berruguete for the *studiolo* of Federico da Montefeltro at the Palazzo Ducale in Urbino (1473-75), and the portraits of Jean

The *sfumato* technique is used to unify the sitter and her natural surroundings in the overall, mellow atmosphere.

Compositionally, the sense of Mona Lisa's immersion in the landscape is heightened by placing her eyes in line with the horizon.

'Mona Lisa': a Model Portrait

Fouquet (1450-60). In Leonardo's oeuvre, Mona Lisa is followed, in decreasing order, by *La Belle Ferronière* (left) and the preparatory cartoon for the portrait of Isabella d'Este (page 14), both of which are at the Louvre, then come *Cecilia Gallerani* (*Lady with an Ermine* (above right) in Cracow, the *Portrait of Ginevra de' Benci* (above) at the National Gallery in Washington, and finally the *Portrait of a Musician* (circa 1485) at the Pinacoteca Ambrosiana in Milan.

In the *Mona Lisa*, Leonardo innovated by placing the model directly in front of a view of nature. True, almost the entire background of his first known portrait, *Ginevra de' Benci*, is filled with a juniper shrub, but this functions as a screen that stops the gaze, whereas in the later work we are given a broad, deep and expansive view of a landscape. All Leonardo's other subjects are portrayed against a neutral background, and Ginevra de'Benci and Mona Lisa are the only figures who look directly at the beholder. With the *Mona Lisa*, therefore, Leonardo was returning to and improving on his early mode of representation.

The solution chosen for the position of Mona Lisa no doubt represents the culmination of thirty years of reflection on the subject, for all the portraits executed by Leonardo after 1480 show him experimenting with the turning movement that is most fully achieved in the *Mona Lisa*. We can see how he gives his figures

Leonardo da Vinci,
La Belle Ferronnière,
1495, oil on wood,
63 x 45 cm,
Paris, Musée du Louvre.

Leonard da Vinci,
Portrait of Ginevra de' Benci, circa 1475,
oil on wood, 38 x 37 cm,
Washington,
National Gallery of Art.

Leonardo da Vinci,
Cecilia Gallerani (Lady with an Ermine)
circa 1490, oil on wood
55 x 40 cm, Cracow,
Czartoryski Museum.

'Mona Lisa': a Model Portrait

greater relief and solves the practical and theoretical difficulty of the genre: conveying the movements of the soul through those of the body. Before the *Mona Lisa*, painters tended to respond to this problem in one of two ways: they either idealised the subject with reference to a type, a physiognomy that clearly conveyed a certain kind of temperament (the 'leonine' warrior, say), or they endowed the model with an attribute whose meaning was easy to decipher (thus, if Cecilia Gallerani holds an ermine, it is because the animal symbolises a purity that would rather die than be sullied, and also because her own surname evokes the Greek for ermine, *galè*).

The Mona Lisa and its artistic context

Strictly speaking, none of the features of this painting was new: not the half-profile position, not the background in which sky and landscape form a balanced composition between columns, not the folded hands in the foreground, not the gaze, directed straight at the beholder, and not even the almost lifelike scale. All these different elements had been tried out individually by Leonardo's predecessors or contemporaries, and especially the Flemish painters. What is extra-ordinary about the *Mona Lisa*, however, is the perfection with which each of these elements is handled, and the way they are successfully synthesised in a single image.

Leonardo da Vinci,
*Portrait of Isabella d'Este
in Profile*, circa 1500,
black chalk on paper,
marked out for transfer,
63 x 46 cm, Paris,
Musée du Louvre.

Raphael,
*Portrait of a Young
Woman*, pen, brown ink,
black chalk,
22.3 x 15.9 cm, Paris,
Musée du Louvre.

Page right:
one of Mona Lisa's
many heirs:
Camille Corot,
Woman with a Pearl,
1840, oil on canvas,
70 x 55 cm, Paris, Musée
du Louvre.

'Mona Lisa': a Model Portrait

MONA LISA BELOW THE SURFACE

Studies carried out by the Centre de Recherche et de Restauration des Musées de France (C2RMF) have shown that Mona Lisa was painted on a single piece of poplar wood 13 millimetres thick, with a very old if undated slit in it 11 centimetres across, whose expansion was neutralised, again at an undetermined but very ancient date, by fixing two clips to the back of the panel.

Recent studies have revealed that this radial, slanting gap predated the network of fine cracks, that the panel, which is now irregularly warped, was never perfectly flat, and that Leonardo had compensated for this in the application of his primer of white lead.

As regards the actual paint, the most recent X-rays have brought to light the artist's hesitancy in tracing certain outlines, notably those of the hands. They have also made it possible to identify most of the pigments and analyse how they were ground, and confirmed the use of semi-opaque glazes made with manganese to heighten the *sfumato* effect.

Aerial perspective also comes from the Flemish school. Once again, though, thanks to his use of *sfumato* technique, which softens the outlines of forms and dilutes them through a mellowing effect obtained by using layers of dark but transparent glazes, Leonardo achieves an exceptional rendering of light and shadow, enveloping the forms and infusing them with that lifelike quality which is the goal of painting. The composition of the *Mona Lisa*, and notably the serpentine form, which is the basis of its originality, was much copied by the painters of the day. Combined with the position of the hands and the naturalness of the pose, these elements were to become the principles of classical grace and elegance – until Mannerism pushed them to their excessive extremes.

Finally, if the *Mona Lisa* represents the techni-cal and formal apogee of the art of portraiture, it also transcends the strict context of painting by virtue of the essential issue that it confronts, an issue that has always been of concern to painters who seek to give their art a philosophical dimension: the representation of time. We need hardly recall that, unlike photography, painting cannot instantaneously capture an expression. Time is of its essence.

The general dialectic of painting lies in the long and patient process of making it, in the interplay between distance and proximity. Beyond 'simple' likeness, what Leonardo was trying to transcribe in this unmoving image destined for posterity, to be looked at through the ages, was the fugacity of passing time. Captured in a smile. ■

FABRICE DOUAR IS AN ART HISTORIAN

Above:
The back of the painting shows the 11 cm slit kept from expanding by two clips. This slit was visible in the sky and in Mona Lisa's hair.

Page right:
The X-ray done in 2004 gave us this ghostly image of Mona Lisa.

The Myth
of the 'Mona Lisa'

While the 'Mona Lisa' is world famous, the origins of its stellar status are relatively obscure. After all, the genius of its creator and the elusive subtlety of his art, however prodigious, can hardly explain the phenomenal cult that has grown up around this masterwork. In fact, the Florentine lady owes her status as the most adulated artwork in the Western World to a thief.

By Jérôme Coignard

Like the aging of a fine wine, the myth of the *Mona Lisa* was the result of a slow and obscure process whose complex chemistry defies formulation. It would be possible, however, to trace its first stirrings to the enthusiastic comments made later in the sixteenth century by Vasari in his *Lives of the Artists*. Does not his description of the painting, in which he mentions the eyelashes and eyebrows, tend to indicate that he had never actually seen it, and was letting himself get carried away by the legend?

Still, the cult of the *Mona Lisa* lay some way ahead. Although the work was part of Louis XIV's Cabinet of paintings at Versailles, *La Joconde*, as she is known in France, was neglected by his successors and we do not find the work mentioned in the catalogue of the Museum Central des Arts (the forerunner of today's Louvre) until 1798. Contrary to what was long believed, the famous smile did not look down on Bonaparte's bedchamber in the Tuileries palace, but on Joséphine's apartments. So much for the legend! It is true that the work was copied on countless occasions, from its inclusion in the collections of Francis I to the eve of the Revolution – Leonardo's apparently seamless, elusive technique offered one of the sternest tests of a painter's skill – but these copies, these bravura exercises, were no more accessible to the public than the original itself.

The making of the myth
It was the invention of lithography that really got things moving. Aubry-Lecomte used this technique to make a copy of the Italian beauty in 1824. While his rather mediocre engraving carelessly reverses the original, the fine texture of the lithographic stone does offer a pleasant approximation of the subtleties of Leonardo's *sfumato*. Above all, the relatively modest cost of the print meant that the image could be made widely available. Mona could at last frequent more modest interiors. The Romantics loved to imagine the lives of the 'masters of yore' and gave us such amusing paintings as 'The King of France Entertaining Mona Lisa to Supper' (Duval-Lecamus, 1825) and 'Leonardo da Vinci Painting the Portrait of Mona Lisa' (Brune-Pagès, 1845). These, too, were popularised by lithography. Here, at last, Leonardo's model was shown from head to toe, in a decor worthy of the comic opera. Many more engravings and lithographs of the *Gioconda* followed. The most remarkable is the one by Ferdinand Gaillard, from around 1887. Combining the techniques of line engraving and etching, it was the result of a hazardous, almost

Clockwise from top left:
Flemish school,
La Joconde, 17th century,
oil on wood, 74 x 57 cm,
Valenciennes,
Musée des Beaux-Arts.

Roman Cieslewicz,
Mona Tse-Tung, 1976,
printed paper and
collage, 51.3 x 41.5 cm,
Vitry-sur-Seine, Musée
d'Art Contemporain.

Claude-Ferdinand Gaillard,
Portrait of Mona Lisa
(*La Joconde*),
1886-87, etching,
42.2 x 33.7 cm, Paris,
Musée du Louvre.

'Mona Lisa Season's
Greetings', photomontage
inspired by the theft of
the painting in 1911 and
its return to the Louvre,
postcard, 1914.

The Myth of the 'Mona Lisa'

Mᶫᶫᵉ POLAIRE
du Vaudeville

Mᶫᶫᵉ Berthe BOVY
de la Comédie-Française

Mᶫᶫᵉ Gabrielle DORZIAT
du Vaudeville

painful undertaking: the attempt to produce something worthy of so eminent a masterpiece in an age when painterly excellence seemed a thing of the past. The luxurious photographs by Goupil and then Braun, glued on cardboard and ready to frame, spread the image of Mona Lisa even further afield.

Paradoxically, this vulgarisation of the painting was accompanied by a certain frustration. The reproductions were, inevitably, disappointing, and, as André Chastel noted, 'as the image became more banal, so the original seemed even more inaccessible and remote'. As the symbol of an unattainable perfection, the object of a desire doomed to remain unsatisfied, the *Mona Lisa* both disturbed and irritated. The making of the myth was truly under way. Then, on 21 August 1911, it received a formidable boost: the painting disappeared from the Louvre. There remained only the frame and nail from which it hung.

The most expensive painting in the world

Early one morning, a fellow named Vincenzo Peruggia had taken the painting under his arm, removed it from its frame and exited the museum without so much as a by-your-leave. When word got out, there was a furore. The public suddenly discovered that the Louvre was not properly guarded; that the wardens, veterans put out to grass by the Ministry of War, were inveterate skivers, men who kept losing their keys and hid their precious litres of red wine in secret staircases or even in historic pieces of furniture; that the two heavy doors of the coach entrance to the Cour Visconti on the Quai du Louvre were frequently left ajar, or even wide open for minutes on end while the cobblestones were being hosed clean.

The Société des Amis du Louvre offered 25,000 francs to anyone who helped track down the painting. An anonymous art lover matched their

selle Polaire and Berthe Bovy to Mistinguett and Gabrielle Dorziat, posed for the camera in their Mona Lisa costumes for a series entitled 'The Smiles We Still Have'. Parisian wit had a field day. Lady Lisa had been knocked off her pedestal and was walking the street. Newspaper vendors were flogging her smile on every corner. It was open season on *La Gioconda*.

A Cubist crime?

One of the most shameful episodes of the police investigation was the arrest of Guillame Apollinaire. The poet was accused of complicity in a 'Cubist plot' to steal the masterpiece. When an artwork as iconic as this mysteriously disappeared, how could the literary and artistic avantgarde possibly fail to be among the prime suspects? Apollinaire was the victim of anonymous denunciations linking him with one Géry-Pieret, a man who had filched from the Louvre a number of 'Phoenician' figurines (in fact, they were Iberian). These had subsequently been sold to Picasso, who greatly admired this little-studied art – indeed, it inspired his *Demoiselles d'Avignon*. When the examining judge brought him face to face with his friend Apollinaire, the painter claimed not to know him. This betrayal can only have added to the bitterness of the poet's time in prison.

As for the real thief, Peruggia, an Italian, he was one of the glaziers who had been employed to put some of the Louvre's most famous paintings under glass in 1910. This modest artisan lived with Mona Lisa in his room on Rue de l'Hôpital Saint-Louis, Paris, for two whole years. Then in 1913 he took a train from the Gare de l'Est and travelled to Basel, whence he continued to Milan and then Florence, where the *Mona Lisa* had been painted. And where he was now arrested. The painting was found wrapped in red vel-

reward. The journal *L'Illustration* promised 10,000 francs to whoever identified the thief, and 50,000 if they brought the painting in to their offices. *Paris-Journal*, finally, offered 10,000 francs. In all, then, 120,000 francs' worth of bounty for a work of art that was now valued at two million. Burglary had made the *Mona Lisa* the most expensive painting in the world.

News of the theft left everyone stunned. Reproduced in countless newspaper articles, the *Mona Lisa* was subjected to innumerable metamorphoses, from kitsch postcards and humorous drawings to outright caricature. One facetious fabric maker invented a punningly named 'Tussor du Louvre' (tussore, a kind of silk, sounding the same as 'tu sors', French for 'you leave') while the stars of the Parisian stage, from Mademoi-

Fernand Léger
Mona Lisa with Keys,
1930, oil on canvas,
91 x 72 cm,
Biot, Musée
Fernand Léger.

Page right:
Andy Warhol,
Mona Lisa,
1963, silkscreen,
New York, The Andy
Warhol Foundation.

The Myth of the 'Mona Lisa'

vet in a wooden crate, along with smocks, brushes, plasterer's tools and even a mandolin. The insignificant Peruggia had set out to return to his native land the painting that, he thought, had been 'stolen from it by Bonaparte', and in so doing had triggered an earthquake of publicity. He was judged in Italy in 1914 and sentenced to a modest year in prison. His story was soon eclipsed by the outbreak of the First World War – in which, as it happens, he fought bravely. The people in his home village of Dumenza, near Como, now called his wife 'la Gioconda' and his daughter 'la Giocondina'. Peruggia died in a Parisian suburb in 1925 at the age of 44. Not one of the newspapers that had splashed his 'sacrilegious act' across its front pages was informed. Peruggia

had been but an unwitting instrument, out of his depth in the affair he had started. But the 'damage' had been done. Never again would it be possible to think of the *Mona Lisa* as simply a painting, or even as simply a supreme masterpiece. The artwork was condemned to live under the patina of its parallel career as a celebrity.

Mona the whiskered lady

Like all spectacular and unsolved crimes, the theft of the *Mona Lisa* was followed by a host of denunciations and fake confessions. Compulsive liars had the police haring down dozens of dead ends. Later, in his 'Portrait of Loyse Baccaris', a story published in 1925, the great writer Gabriele D'Annunzio would accuse himself of having ordered the theft: "I remember that when the sublime thief of the *Mona Lisa* brought the panel wrapped in an old stable blanket to my retreat on the moors, I remember how I began to loathe the limp hands of Mona Lisa'.

The confession met with indifference. But when, in 1919, Marcel Duchamp drew a moustache and a goatee on a postcard of the *Mona Lisa*, thus creating one of his most famous assisted readymades, titled *L.H.O.O.Q.*, it was a decisive moment in the emergence of modern art. Total profanation. For centuries the symbol and epitome of 'great painting', the *Mona Lisa* was now about to be deformed, recycled and scorned by generations of artists. From Fernand Léger to Raymond Hains, from Andy Warhol to Robert Filliou and from Pol Bury to René Monory, the *Mona Lisa* was to become one of the touchstones of modernity. Adulated or vilified, it hardly mattered: Leonardo's painting had become an absolute reference, consecrated by the adoration of the masses. Indispensable, or unavoidable. ■

JÉRÔME COIGNARD IS AN ART HISTORIAN

Robert Filliou,
'The Mona Lisa on the Stairs', 1968, cardboard, broom, bucket and floor cloth, Saint-Etienne, Musée d'Art Moderne.

Page right:
Marcel Duchamp,
L.H.O.O.Q., 1919,
lithograph, Rome,
Galleria Pictogramma.

La Joconde.

L.H.O.O.Q.

The Salle des États

A Florentine among Venetians

The architecture of the room has been entirely rethought in order to more effectively showcase the 'Mona Lisa' and Veronese's huge 'Wedding at Cana', and to improve their visibility for visitors. A new glass roof provides overhead lighting for these two masterworks and for the fifty paintings from the Venetian School that surround them.

BY JEAN HABERT

The great ensemble of buildings (*pavillons*) linked by wings and separated by courtyards that we know as the Louvre came into its present form in 1857, in the reign of Napoleon III. This 'Nouveau Louvre' was the outstanding example of the Second Empire's Grand Style. The 'Salle des Etats', which occupies the whole upper floor of the Pavillon of the same name, running from north to south between the Salon Denon and the Grande Galerie, was built between 1852 and 1857 by Hector Lefuel. The Daru, Denon and Mollien rooms served as its vestibules and entrance. Also known as the 'Imperial Room', it was used for the regime's official ceremonies and, at the opening of each legislative session, was where the various state bodies (*corps d'état*) assembled in the presence of the Emperor. Lit on both sides by a triple row of windows, its ceiling featured a set of paintings by Charles-Louis Muller (1815-92) celebrating 'The Glory of France' while, above the doors, the artist's works illustrated the triumphs of Caesar and Charlemagne.

From French to Italian painting

With the advent of the Third Republic, the hall lost its function and was made available to the Musée du Louvre, whose architect, Edmond Guillaume, transformed it into a space for modern French painting. Lefuel and Muller's decor was almost completely destroyed: the doors and windows were taken out, leaving only a door at each end of the room. The vaulted ceiling was replaced by glass panels to provide overhead light and the sloping sides were adorned with stucco works representing the main French painters, alternating with allegories of ancient and modern France. This 'Salon Carré' (square room) housing French painting of the nineteenth century (including works by Ingres, David, Delacroix and Manet) was inaugurated in 1886 and retained this function until the Second Word War.

After the War, this second architectural arrangement was also destroyed and the room was recast by Haffner to house Venetian painting from the sixteenth century. This new space

The *Mona Lisa* is presented alone on a picture wall three quarters of the way along the Salle des Etats, facing *The Wedding at Cana* by Veronese. On the other side of the wall, Venetian paintings from the early sixteenth century surround Titian's *Concert Champêtre*. On the walls around it hang Venetian paintings from the second half of the century.

Double page over: Caliari Paolo Veronese, *The Wedding at Cana*, 1563, oil on canvas, 677 x 994 cm, Paris, Musée du Louvre.

inaugurated in 1952 still had the glazed ceiling from before, but on the walls the side panels had been replaced by a Greek-style orthogonal pattern in accordance with the taste of the day, and at the northern end a big picture wall had been built for Veronese's *The Wedding at Cana*. The *Mona Lisa* was installed in this room in 1966. However, this third incarnation of the Salon Carré was soon judged unsatisfactory as a gallery for paintings because of its poor lighting, awkward crowd flows, echoing acoustic and lack of air conditioning.

A new showcase for the *Mona Lisa* and *The Wedding at Cana*

It took several decades for the arrangement to be replaced with a new decor designed by Lorenzo Piqueras, who won the competition organised in 1999 for an improved layout. Aiming to render the movements of visitors more fluid, the new single-space design allowed

for frontal viewing of Leonardo's and Veronese's masterpieces. The latter, the biggest painting in the Louvre (6.77 m high, 9.94 wide), occupies the wall delimiting the Grande Galerie on the other side, 28 metres from the *Mona Lisa*. This distance affords the proper distance for viewing the painting, in accordance with its original conception for the refectory of the monastery of San Giorgio Maggiore in Venice. As for the *Mona Lisa*, the Louvre's most famous painting, its presentation needed to be perfectly secure and at the same time sufficiently open to allow access to the thousands of admirers who come to pay homage each day. For this reason it is installed in a shallow glass case which makes it easier to light it and control its temperature and humidity, placed some three-quarters of the way up the room. Mona Lisa's gaze carries towards the Grande Galerie, where the other paintings by Leonardo da Vinci are presented in chronological order: *The Virgin of the*

Tiziano Vecellio, known as Titian, *Le Concert Champêtre*, circa 1509, oil on canvas, 105 x 136 cm, Paris, Musée du Louvre.

Lorenzo Lotto, *The Adoration of the Infant Jesus*, 1536-37, oil on canvas, 150 x 237 cm, Paris, Musée du Louvre.

Rocks (1483-86), *The Virgin, Child and Saint Anne* (circa 1510) and *Saint John the Baptist* (circa 1516-1517).

Masterpieces from Venice

Some fifty Venetian paintings from the sixteenth century are also presented in the renovated Salle des Etats. The Cinquecento was a golden age for the Serenissima, when the power of Venice was its peak and its school of painting also at its apogee. The Venetian style represents a unique synthesis of northern and southern influences, characterised by the love of colour that Venice inherited from Byzantium. Giorgione was the great initiator of modern Venetian painting, the creator of an intimate, natural style. Titian, his closest collaborator, succeeded him as the leading painter. The masterpieces that he painted through to 1515 constitute the foundation of Venetian or 'chromatic' classicism, and an impressive number of them are to be found in the Louvre, notably the *Concert Champêtre, The Entombment, A Woman at Her Toilet, Man with a Glove* and *The Pilgrims of Emmaus.* After 1540 Venetian painting moved towards Mannerism, although it never sacrificed its taste for naturalness. Titian's influence was immense, and inspired artists such as Bassano (whose *Deposition of Christ* and *Two Hunting Dogs Tethered to a Stump* can be admired in the Louvre), Tintoretto (*Suzanna at Her Bath*) and of course Veronese (*Jupiter Striking Down the Vices, Countess Nani*). After the early death of Veronese in 1588, followed by Jacopo Bassano 1592 and Tintoretto in 1594, the golden age of Venetian painting entered its sunset years with the art of Jacopo's son Leandro Bassano and Palma the Younger (the great nephew of Palma the Elder, and a student of Titian and Tintoretto). ∎

JEAN HABERT IS HEAD CURATOR IN CHARGE OF 16TH-CENTURY VENETIAN PAINTING AT THE MUSÉE DU LOUVRE.

Jacopo Palma Vecchio,
The Adoration of the Shepherds,
1520, oil on canvas,
140 x 210 cm,
Paris, Musée du Louvre.

Jacopo Bassano,
The Deposition,
circa 1580-1582,
oil on canvas,
154 x 225 cm,
Paris, Musée du Louvre.

About Mona Lisa...
A Compact Anthology

It is the smile that launched a million paragraphs, many full of praise for Leonardo's masterpiece, others expressing amazement at Mona Lisa's mythical smile, and yet others venting irritation at a cult gone too far. These pages offer a modest if choice selection from writers, poets and art historians.

Anyone wishing to see the degree to which art can imitate Nature can easily understand this from the head, for here Leonardo reproduced all the details that can be painted with subtlety. The eyes have the lustre and moisture always seen in living people, while around them are the lashes and all the reddish tones which cannot be produced without the greatest care. The eyebrows could not be more natural, for they represent the way the hair grows in the skin – –thicker in some places and thinner in others, following the pores of the skin. The nose seems lifelike with its beautiful pink and tender nostrils. The mouth, with its opening joining the red of the lips to the flesh of the face, seems to be real flesh rather than paint. Anyone who looked very attentively at the hollow of her throat would see her pulse beating: to tell the truth, it can be said that portrait was painted in a way that would cause every brave artist to tremble and fear, whoever he might be. Since Mona Lisa was very beautiful, Leonardo employed this technique: while he was painting her portrait, he had musicians who played or sang and clowns who would always make her merry in order to drive away her melancholy, which painting often brings to portraits. And in this portrait by Leonardo, there is a smile so pleasing that it seems more divine than human, and it was considered a wondrous thing that it was as lively as the smile of the living original.'
Giorgio Vasari, *Vite dei più eccellenti architetti, pittori e scultori italiani (The Lives of the Artists),* **Florence, 1550.**

'The sinuous mouth, turning up at the corners, under purplish half-light, mocks you so gently, with such grace and superiority, that you feel as shy as a schoolboy standing before a duchess.'
Théophile Gautier, *Les Dieux et les Demi-Dieux de la peinture,* **Paris, 1864.**

'O Mona Lisa, so wondrously radiant
With the glow of your soulful forms,
With your gentle, mysterious mouth
With the splendour of your dream–heavy eyelids,
In my questions how I wish to devote to you
The life with which you overwhelm me.'
Hugo von Hofmannsthal,
Der Thor und der Tod, **1893.**

'*La Gioconda* is, in the truest sense, Leonardo's masterpiece, the revealing instance of his mode of thought and work. [...] She is older than the rocks among which she sits; like the vampire, she has been dead many times, and learned the secrets of the grave; and has been a diver in deep seas, and keeps their fallen day about her; and

trafficked for strange webs with Eastern merchants: and, as Leda, was the mother of Helen of Troy, and, as Saint Anne, the mother of Mary; and all this has been to her but as the sound of lyres and flutes, and lives only in the delicacy with which it has moulded the changing lineaments, and tinged the eyelids and the hands.'
Walter Pater, *Studies in the History of the Renaissance,* 1873.

'The "Mona Lisa smile" is without thought. With this smile she is saying: I am thinking of nothing. Leonardo is thinking for me.'
Paul Valéry, *Cahiers,* 1906-1907.

'The fame of Mona Lisa, further increased by the sensational theft, has become tedious.'
Max Friedländer, *Landscape. Portrait. Still Life,* Oxford, 1949.

'Before Leonardo, portraits lacked mystery; artists represented only soulless exteriors or, if they did try to convey the soul, tried to communicate it to beholders through gesture, through symbolic objects, through inscriptions. Only the *Mona Lisa* exudes this enigma: the soul is present but inaccessible.'
Charles de Tolnay, «Remarques sur *La Joconde*», in *Revue des Arts,* Paris, 1951.

'In 1919, I was back in Paris, where the Dada movement had just emerged. Tristan Tzara, who had come from Switzerland, where the movement got going in 1916, joined the group that had formed around André Breton in Paris. Picabia and I had already manifested our sympathy for Dada. This Mona Lisa with a moustache and goatee is a combination of readymade and Dadaist iconoclasm. The original, I mean the original readymade, is a cheap 8 x 5 (inch) print on the back of which I wrote five initials which, when spoken out loud in French, form a very risqué joke about the *Mona Lisa.*'
Marcel Duchamp, *Duchamp du signe, writings of Marcel Duchamp,* 1976.

'Mona Lisa is smiling because all the people who drew whiskers on her are dead.'
André Malraux, *La Tête d'obsidienne,* 1974.

'The industry of loose prints and postcards has made the *Mona Lisa* the archetype of the artwork that reigns over the museum, that forms its precious heart and, in a word, thus justifies the institution.'
André Chastel, *L'Illustre incomprise, 1988.*

'Kenneth Clark, the great Leonardo da Vinci specialist, a very serious man and one of the finest art historians of the mid-twentieth century […] wrote that Mona Lisa looks like an underwater goddess. […] What is there going on in this painting to make serious people, museum directors and learned figures, say such things?'

'And then there is the smile […] In fact, it was Leonardo who invented the idea of a portrait with a smile. There is no smiling portrait before the *Mona Lisa*, with the exception of Antonello da Messina's *Portrait of an Unknown Man* […] Mona Lisa is smiling because her husband, Francesco del Giocondo, commissioned her painting from the greatest painter of the day, Leonardo da Vinci. And why did the husband commission her portrait? Because she had given him two handsome children, two male heirs, and because as a result they had to move house in Florence. We know all that: the mystery of the *Mona Lisa* lies not in what has been spun around it, but in the painting itself. The husband bought another palazzo, he extended his house and offered his wife a portrait of herself by the maestro Leonardo. She was never to receive it; Leonardo kept it for himself. It is, in any case, a picture of happiness, in which a young woman of twenty-two or twenty-three […] is honoured by [her husband's] love through this portrait.'
Daniel Arasse, *Histoires de peintures,* 2004.

Practical Guide

SOME DATES

- **1503-1506** According to Giorgio Vasari (1511-74), a Florentine painter and author of a biography of the artist published in 1550, Leonardo is working on the portrait of *Mona Lisa*.
- **1506** Leonardo leaves Florence for Milan, taking the unfinished painting with him.
- **1516** Leonardo travels to France at the invitation of Francis I, again with the painting. He probably goes back to it at a later date.
- **1518** Francis I buys the painting from Salaï, one of Leonardo's two heirs.
- **1550** Vasari notes that *the Mona Lisa* is in Francis I's château at Fontainebleau.
- **1650** The work is noted at the Louvre. Then, in the late 17th and 18th centuries at Versailles.
- **1798** *Mona Lisa* is transferred to the Museum Central des Arts, housed in the Louvre's Salon Carré.
- **1799** Napoleon installs the painting in Joséphine's apartments in the Tuileries.
- **1804** *Mona Lisa* is moved back to the Louvre (for good, as it turns out). The painting is hung in the Grande Galerie.

- **1911** An Italian, Vincenzo Peruggia, steals the painting in order to return it to his country.
- **1913** On 11 December, after being exhibited in Florence, Rome and Milan, *The Mona Lisa* returns to Paris.
- **1914-1918** During the First World War the Louvre keeps its masterpieces safe in the Couvent des Jacobins in Toulouse.
- **1939-1945** During the Second, *The Mona Lisa* is kept in five different hiding places around France.
- **1956** A young Bolivian, Ugo Unganza Villegas, throws a stone at the painting. Only *The Mona Lisa*'s left elbow is damaged. From now on, the work is kept behind reinforced glass.
- **1962** On board the liner *France* the *Mona Lisa* travels to America where, in the space of three months, it is seen by two million visitors in Washington and New York.
- **1974** *The Mona Lisa* takes the plane to Japan where 20,000 people a day flock to see it.